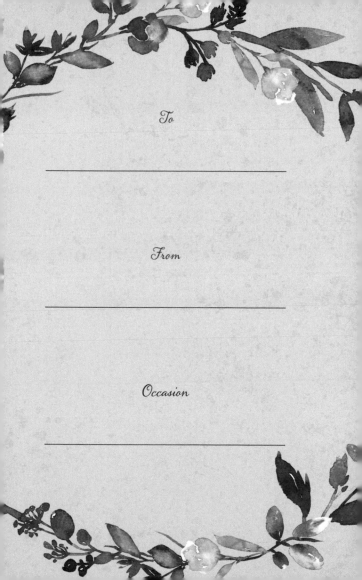

To

_____

From

_____

Occasion

_____

a bouquet of

Heartfelt Prayers

to give you strength

Tyndale House Publishers, Inc.

CAROL STREAM, ILLINOIS

O God, thou art my God; early will I seek
thee: my soul thirsteth for thee, my flesh
longeth for thee in a dry and thirsty land,
where no water is.

PSALM 63:1, KJV

More things
are wrought by
prayer than this
world dreams of.

ALFRED, LORD TENNYSON

If I don't hear from
God in prayer,
*maybe I'm making
too much noise.*

LONNI COLLINS PRATT

The Spirit helps us in our weakness. We do not know what we ought to pray for, but the Spirit himself intercedes for us through wordless groans.

ROMANS 8:26, NIV

O LORD, hear me as I pray. . . . Listen to my cry for help, my King and my God, for I pray to no one but you. Listen to my voice in the morning, LORD. Each morning I bring my requests to you and wait expectantly. . . . Lead me in the right path, O LORD. . . . Make your way plain for me to follow.

PSALM 5:1-3, 8

Is any among you suffering? Let him pray. Is anyone cheerful? Let him sing psalms.

JAMES 5:13, NKJV

Rejoice in our *confident hope.*

Be patient in trouble, and keep on praying.

ROMANS 12:12

May the strength of God pilot us.

May the power of God preserve us.

May the wisdom of God instruct us.

May the hand of God protect us.

May the way of God direct us.

ST. PATRICK

God can be everywhere at once, heeding the prayers of all who call out in the name of Christ; performing the mighty miracles that keep the stars in their places, and the plants bursting up through the earth, and the fish swimming in the sea. There is no limit to God.

BILLY GRAHAM

Bend down,
O LORD, and hear
my prayer;
answer me, for
I need your help.

PSALM 86:1

Don't pray when you feel like it. Have an appointment with the Lord and keep it.

CORRIE TEN BOOM

Mary said, "My soul magnifies the Lord,
and my spirit rejoices in God my Savior,
for he has looked on the humble estate of
his servant. For behold, from now on all
generations will call me blessed; for he who
is mighty has done great things for me,
and holy is his name."

LUKE 1:46-49, ESV

We pray always for you, that our God would count you worthy of this calling, and fulfil all the good pleasure of his goodness, and the work of faith with power: That the name of our Lord Jesus Christ may be glorified in you, and ye in him, according to the grace of our God and the Lord Jesus Christ.

2 THESSALONIANS 1:11-12, KJV

Lord, we come before you
today with reverence.
Teach us to trust
and hope only
in you.

ALFRED, LORD TENNYSON

Whatever things
you ask in prayer,
*believing,
you will
receive.*

MATTHEW 21:22, NKJV

Keep on asking, and you will receive what you ask for. Keep on seeking, and you will find. Keep on knocking, and the door will be opened to you. For everyone who asks, receives. Everyone who seeks, finds. And to everyone who knocks, the door will be opened.

MATTHEW 7:7-8

Nothing lies beyond the reach of prayer except that which lies outside the will of God.

DUNCAN CAMPBELL

Give your burdens to the
LORD, and he will

take care of you.

PSALM 55:22

When I shut up the heavens so that there
is no rain, or command locusts to devour the
land or send a plague among my people, if
my people, who are called by my name, will
humble themselves and pray and seek my
face and turn from their wicked ways, then
I will hear from heaven, and I will forgive
their sin and will heal their land.

2 CHRONICLES 7:13-14, NIV

Instead of asking him to give the things
for which we pray, all that we need to ask
from God is this: Show us the way.

JAMES A. BOWMAN

Prayer is cooperation with God—not getting what I want, but learning what he wants.

ELISABETH ELLIOT GREN

The heavenly

Father

will always be there when
you seek Him and find
Him at the altar of prayer.

HELEN STEINER RICE

This is the confidence we have in
approaching God: that if we ask anything
according to his will, he hears us. And if
we know that he hears us whatever we
ask-we know that we have what we asked
of him.

1 JOHN 5:14-15, NIV

Our Father which art in heaven, Hallowed be thy name. Thy kingdom come, Thy will be done in earth, as it is in heaven. Give us this day our daily bread. And forgive us our debts, as we forgive our debtors. And lead us not into temptation, but deliver us from evil: For thine is the kingdom, and the power, and the glory, for ever. Amen.

MATTHEW 6:9-13, KJV

The LORD has
heard my plea;
the LORD will
answer my prayer.

PSALM 6:9

O God, be my guide.
Restore myself to
thee, through
Jesus Christ.

ST. AUGUSTINE

Show me your unfailing love in wonderful ways. By your mighty power you rescue those who seek refuge from their enemies. Guard me as you would guard your own eyes. Hide me in the shadow of your wings.

PSALM 17:7-8

I will answer them before they even call to me. While they are still talking about their needs, I will go ahead and answer their prayers!

ISAIAH 65:24

Devote yourselves to
prayer with an
alert mind and a thankful heart.

COLOSSIANS 4:2

Ask me and
I will tell you
remarkable
secrets you do
not know
about things
to come.

JEREMIAH 33:3

And now unto him who is able to keep us from falling and lift us from the dark valley of despair to the bright mountain of hope, from the midnight of desperation to the daybreak of joy; to him be power and authority, for ever and ever.

MARTIN LUTHER KING, JR.

In my distress
I called to the
LORD, and he
answered me.

JONAH 2:2, NIV

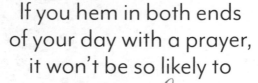

If you hem in both ends
of your day with a prayer,
it won't be so likely to

*unravel in
the middle.*

UNKNOWN

As the deer longs for streams of water, so
I long for you, O God. I thirst for God, the
living God. . . . But each day the LORD pours
his unfailing love upon me, and through each
night I sing his songs, praying to God who
gives me life.

PSALM 42:1-2, 8

[An angel said,] "Daniel, you are very precious to God, so listen carefully to what I have to say to you. . . . Don't be afraid, Daniel. Since the first day you began to pray for understanding and to humble yourself before your God, your request has been heard in heaven. I have come in answer to your prayer."

DANIEL 10:11-12

The effectual fervent
prayer of a righteous man
availeth much.

JAMES 5:16, KJV

The LORD is
close
to all who call on him,
yes, to all who call on
him in truth.

PSALM 145:18

Such gracious access is granted to us even
by the King of heaven, and day and night
His ready hearing and His help are within
the reach of all that come to Him.

DWIGHT L. MOODY

Now all glory to God, who is able, through his mighty power at work within us, to accomplish infinitely more than we might ask or think. Glory to him in the church and in Christ Jesus through all generations forever and ever! Amen.

EPHESIANS 3:20-21

How can I bear to be silent when your daily mercies are all around me singing of your love?

CHARLES SPURGEON

God is the only source of real power and the only enduring fountainhead of love and companionship.

BILLY GRAHAM

I pray that your love will overflow more
and more, and that you will keep on growing
in knowledge and understanding. For I want
you to understand what really matters, so
that you may live pure and blameless lives
until the day of Christ's return.

PHILIPPIANS 1:9-10

Lord, there are times when the only stability in the world is the Cross of Christ. So, to that Cross we turn, praying that you'd give us the courage to do only what needs to be done in your eyes, through your power.

LARRY BURKETT

We put our hope
in the LORD.

He is our help
and our shield.

———

PSALM 33:20

I desire then
that in every place
the men should pray,
lifting holy hands

*without anger
or quarreling.*

1 TIMOTHY 2:8, ESV

I urge you, first of all, to pray for all people. Ask God to help them; intercede on their behalf, and give thanks for them. Pray this way for kings and all who are in authority so that we can live peaceful and quiet lives marked by godliness and dignity. This is good and pleases God our Savior, who wants everyone to be saved and to understand the truth.

1 TIMOTHY 2:1-4

Father God, with
thee there is light.
. . . . Thy ways are
past understanding,
but thou knowest
the way for me.

DIETRICH BONHOEFFER

Let me be slow to do my will, prompt to obey, and

keep me, guide me, use me, Lord, just for today.

UNKNOWN

He regarded their affliction, when He heard
their cry; and for their sake He remembered
His covenant, and relented according to the
multitude of His mercies.

PSALM 106:44-45, NKJV

We ask God to give you complete knowledge of his will and to give you spiritual wisdom and understanding. Then the way you live will always honor and please the Lord, and your lives will produce every kind of good fruit. All the while, you will grow as you learn to know God better and better.

COLOSSIANS 1:9-10

You, Lord, are forgiving
and good, abounding in love
to all who call to you.

PSALM 86:5, NIV

It is good to give

thanks

to the LORD, to sing
praises to the Most High.

PSALM 92:1

Divine Master, grant that I may not so much seek to be consoled . . . as to console, to be loved . . . as to love, for it is in giving that we receive, it is in pardoning . . . that we are pardoned. it is in dying . . . that we are born to eternal life.

ST. FRANCIS OF ASSISI

You are wonderful beyond describing it.
And yet you love me. . . . And nonetheless,
you bend your boundless being, your
infinity, into space and time, into things
and into history, to find me, to preserve
my life.

WALT WANGERIN JR.

I urge you . . . in view of God's *mercy*, to offer your bodies as a *living sacrifice*, holy and pleasing to *God*.

ROMANS 12:1, NIV

I entrust my
spirit into your
hand. Rescue me,
LORD, for you are a
faithful God.

PSALM 31:5

If I fail to spend two hours in prayer each morning, the devil gets the victory through the day. I have so much business I cannot get on without three hours daily in prayer.

MARTIN LUTHER

I am your servant; deal with me in
unfailing love, and teach me your decrees.
Give discernment to me, your servant;
then I will understand your laws.

PSALM 119:124-125

Lord, where we are
wrong, make us willing
to change;

where we are
right, make us
easy to live with.

———

PETER MARSHALL

No one is holy like
the LORD!
There is no
one besides
you; there is
no Rock like
our God.

1 SAMUEL 2:2

Eternal God, the light of the minds that know you, the life of the souls that love you, help us so to know you that we may truly love you, so to love you that we may truly serve you.

ST. AUGUSTINE

I pray to you,
O LORD. I say,
"You are my place of
refuge. You are all
I really want in life."

PSALM 142:5

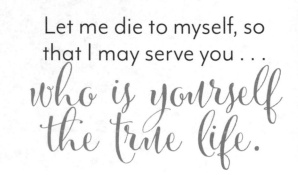

Let me die to myself, so
that I may serve you . . .
*who is yourself
the true life.*

TERESA OF AVILA

King David went in and sat before the LORD and prayed, "Who am I, O Sovereign LORD, and what is my family, that you have brought me this far? . . . How great you are, O Sovereign LORD! There is no one like you. We have never even heard of another God like you!

2 SAMUEL 7:18, 22

You have heard the law that says, "Love your neighbor" and hate your enemy. But I say, love your enemies! Pray for those who persecute you! In that way, you will be acting as true children of your Father in heaven. For he gives his sunlight to both the evil and the good, and he sends rain on the just and the unjust alike.

MATTHEW 5:43-45

Be exalted, O God,
above the heavens; let your
glory be over all the earth.

PSALM 57:5, NIV

Search for the LORD
and for his

strength;

continually seek him.
Remember the wonders
he has performed.

1 CHRONICLES 16:11-12

A prayerless Christian is a powerless Christian. Jesus Christ spent many hours in prayer. Sometimes He spent the night on a mountaintop in solitary communion with God the Father. If He felt that He had to pray, how much more do we need to pray?

BILLY GRAHAM

It is in the place of prayer that God
enlightens the soul, making it see his
grandeur and majesty. . . . Contemplation
is nothing else but a secret, peaceful, and
loving infusion of God, which, if admitted,
will set the soul on fire with the spirit
of love.

ST. JOHN OF THE CROSS

Take *control* of
what I say, O LORD,
and *guard* my lips.

PSALM 141:3

Deal well with me,
O Sovereign LORD,
for the sake of your
own reputation! . . .
You are so faithful
and good.

PSALM 109:21

Lord, make me an instrument of thy peace.

Where there is hatred, let me sow love;

Where there is injury, pardon;

Where there is doubt, faith;

Where there is despair, hope;

Where there is darkness, light;

Where there is sadness, joy.

ST. FRANCIS OF ASSISI

I pray that you, being rooted and established in love, may have power, together with all the Lord's holy people, to grasp how wide and long and high and deep is the love of Christ, and to know this love that surpasses knowledge–that you may be filled to the measure of all the fullness of God.

EPHESIANS 3:17-19, NIV

Teach us, Holy Father,
to hope in your name.
Open our inward
eyes to recognize you.

ST. CLEMENT OF ROME

Glorious God, it is
the flame of my life
to worship thee,

*the crown and
glory of my soul
to adore thee.*

PURITAN PRAYER

God desires that Christians be concerned
and burdened for a lost world. If we
pray this kind of prayer, an era of peace
may come to the world and the hordes of
wickedness may be turned back.

BILLY GRAHAM

God forbid that
I should sin against
the LORD in
ceasing to pray
for you.

1 SAMUEL 12:23, KJV

Blessed Father! Let us and
our children be Thine
*wholly and
forever. Amen.*

ANDREW MURRAY

Among the gods there is none like you,
Lord; no deeds can compare with yours. All
the nations you have made will come and
worship before you, Lord; they will bring
glory to your name. For you are great and
do marvelous deeds; you alone are God.

PSALM 86:8-10, NIV

The tax collector stood at a distance and dared not even lift his eyes to heaven as he prayed. Instead, he beat his chest in sorrow, saying, "O God, be merciful to me, for I am a sinner." I tell you, this sinner, not the Pharisee, returned home justified before God. For those who exalt themselves will be humbled, and those who humble themselves will be exalted.

LUKE 18:13-14

Perhaps the single most overlooked discipline in the Christian life (and among the most difficult) is consistent prayer. Prevailing prayer. Ongoing, unceasing prayer.

CHARLES R. SWINDOLL

If you look for me
wholeheartedly,
you will find me.

JEREMIAH 29:13

Peace be with you, dear brothers and sisters, and may God the Father and the Lord Jesus Christ give you love with faithfulness. May God's grace be eternally upon all who love our Lord Jesus Christ.

EPHESIANS 6:23-24

We may make requests, but never insist on having our own way. We may pray in simple, childlike faith; urgently, persistently. But we must always pray, "Thy will be done."

RUTH BELL GRAHAM

I will praise
you as long as I live,
lifting up my
hands to
you in prayer.

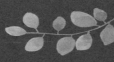

PSALM 63:4

Omnipotent God,
grant to us peace
in our time.

HENRY FOTHERGILL CHORLEY

I will thank you, LORD, among all the people.
I will sing your praises among the nations.
For your unfailing love is higher than the
heavens. Your faithfulness reaches to the
clouds. Be exalted, O God, above the highest
heavens. May your glory shine over all
the earth.

PSALM 108:3-5

Keep watch, dear Lord, with those who work,
or watch, or weep this night, and give your
angels charge over those who sleep. Tend
the sick, Lord Christ; give rest to the weary,
bless the dying, soothe the suffering, pity
the afflicted, shield the joyous and all for
your love's sake.

UNKNOWN

You, O Lord, are a
God of compassion and
mercy, slow to get angry
and filled with
unfailing love
and faithfulness.

PSALM 86:15

I will thank the LORD because he is just; I will sing praise to the name

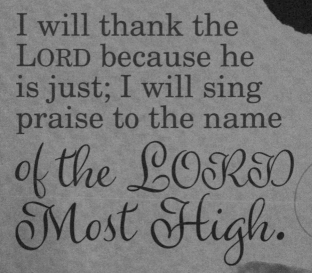

of the LORD Most High.

PSALM 7:17

Lord, shine in me and so be in me that all with whom I come in contact may know thy presence in my soul. Let them look up and see no longer me but only Jesus.

JOHN HENRY NEWMAN

The LORD detests the sacrifice of the wicked, but the prayer of the upright pleases him.

PROVERBS 15:8, NIV

A single grateful thought
raised to heaven is the

most perfect
prayer.

GOTTHOLD EPHRAIM LESSING

God of All, Almighty God, your wisdom
abounds in the glory of creation and is
beyond our understanding.

OCCASIONAL SERVICES: A COMPANION TO LUTHERAN

BOOK OF WORSHIP

Answer me quickly, LORD; my spirit fails. Do not hide your face from me or I will be like those who go down to the pit. Let the morning bring me word of your unfailing love, for I have put my trust in you. Show me the way I should go, for to you I entrust my life.

PSALM 143:7-8, NIV

O heavenly Father,
so frame this heart of mine,
that I may ever delight to
live according to thy will.

GEORGE WASHINGTON

Restore to me the *joy* of your salvation, and make me willing to obey you.

PSALM 51:12

My faith looks up to thee, thou Lamb of Calvary, Savior divine! Now hear me while I pray; take all my guilt away. O let me from this day be wholly thine!

RAY PALMER

I always thank my God as I remember you
in my prayers, because I hear about your
love for all his holy people and your faith
in the Lord Jesus.

PHILEMON 1:4-5, NIV

Eternal
Father, Spirit, Word,
I give praise to the Lord
of my salvation.

ST. PATRICK

Teach us, good Lord, to serve you as you deserve; to give and not to count the cost.

IGNATIUS OF LOYOLA

[Jesus] went on a little farther and bowed with his face to the ground, praying, "My Father! If it is possible, let this cup of suffering be taken away from me. Yet I want your will to be done, not mine."

MATTHEW 26:39

If any of you lacks wisdom, let him ask God, who gives generously to all without reproach, and it will be given him. But let him ask in faith, with no doubting, for the one who doubts is like a wave of the sea that is driven and tossed by the wind. For that person must not suppose that he will receive anything from the Lord; he is a double-minded man, unstable in all his ways.

JAMES 1:5-8, ESV

Lord, I seek refuge in you. Help me to see my circumstances clearly, **and to remember that you're in control.**

PATSY CLAIRMONT

Have mercy
on me, Lord,
for I call
to you all
day long.

PSALM 86:3, NIV

God my Savior, please show me your ways and teach me your paths. Help me to submit my choices and decisions to you, and to let your truth guide me and teach me. In the name of Jesus Christ, I pray. Amen.

JOSH McDOWELL

You are the God who
saves me. . . .
May my prayer come
before you; turn your
ear to my cry.

PSALM 88:1-2, NIV

God's promises are intended
not to supersede,
but to excite and
encourage our prayers

MATTHEW HENRY

All heaven will praise your great wonders,
LORD. . . . For who in all of heaven can
compare with the LORD? . . . The highest
angelic powers stand in awe of God. He is
far more awesome than all who surround his
throne. O LORD God of Heaven's Armies! Where
is there anyone as mighty as you, O LORD?
You are entirely faithful.

PSALM 89:5-8

My prayer is not for the world, but for
those you have given me, because they
belong to you. All who are mine belong to
you, and you have given them to me, so they
bring me glory. . . . Holy Father, you have
given me your name; now protect them by
the power of your name so that they will
be united just as we are.

JOHN 17:9-11

Have mercy on us and forgive us; that we may delight in your will, and walk in your ways, to the glory of your Name.

THE BOOK OF COMMON PRAYER

This is what the LORD,
the God of your
ancestor David, says:
I have

heard

your prayer.

2 KINGS 20:5

"Blessing and honor and glory and power
belong to the one sitting on the throne and
to the Lamb forever and ever." And the four
living beings said, "Amen!"

REVELATION 5:13-14

Thou Lord, alone, art all thy children need
and there is none beside; in thee the blest
abide, fountain of life and all-abounding
grace, our source, our center, and our
dwelling place!

MADAME GUYON

When you stand *praying*, if you hold anything against anyone, *forgive* them, so that your *Father* in *heaven* may forgive you your sins.

MARK 11:25, NIV

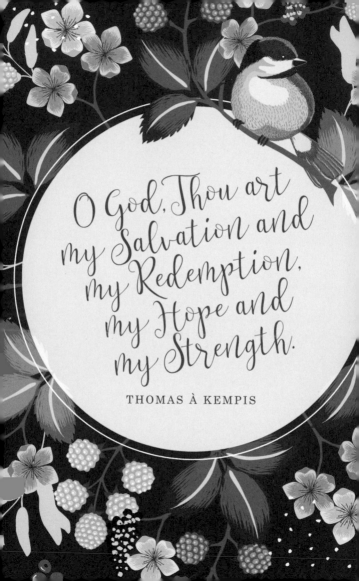

O God, Thou art my Salvation and my Redemption, my Hope and my Strength.

THOMAS À KEMPIS

Rescue me from the mud; don't let me sink any deeper! Save me from those who hate me, and pull me from these deep waters. Don't let the floods overwhelm me, or the deep waters swallow me, or the pit of death devour me. Answer my prayers, O LORD, for your unfailing love is wonderful. Take care of me, for your mercy is so plentiful.

PSALM 69:14-16

What other nation is so great as to have their gods near them the way the L ORD our God is near us whenever we pray to him?

DEUTERONOMY 4:7, NIV

Never stop
praying.

1 THESSALONIANS 5:17

You are my God,
and I will praise you!

You are
my God,
and I will
exalt you!

PSALM 118:28

What a difference it might make if each day, as newscasts conclude, a great wave of prayer could ascend to God from across the country on behalf of those in trouble and those making trouble!

RUTH BELL GRAHAM

If two of you on earth agree about anything they ask for, it will be done for them by my Father in heaven.

MATTHEW 18:19, NIV

You are the Lord who lives,
the rock of ages,
*the fountain of
living waters.*

PURITAN PRAYER

Jabez called on the God of Israel saying, "Oh, that You would bless me indeed, and enlarge my territory, that Your hand would be with me, and that You would keep me from evil, that I may not cause pain!" So God granted him what he requested.

1 CHRONICLES 4:10, NKJV

Teach me your ways, O LORD, that I may live according to your truth! Grant me purity of heart, so that I may honor you. With all my heart I will praise you, O Lord my God. I will give glory to your name forever, for your love for me is very great. You have resoucd me from the depths of death.

PSALM 86:11-13

O God, hold forth
Thy light before me;
recall me from my
wanderings.

ST. AUGUSTINE

I pray that out of his

glorious riches

he may strengthen you
with power through his
Spirit in your inner being.

EPHESIANS 3:16, NIV

We also pray that you will be strengthened
with all his glorious power so you will have
all the endurance and patience you need.
May you be filled with joy, always thanking
the Father.

COLOSSIANS 1:11-12

May you always be filled with the fruit
of your salvation-the righteous character
produced in your life by Jesus Christ-
for this will bring much glory and praise
to God.

PHILIPPIANS 1:11

You are the God
and Father of men,
the source of all
truth and goodness
and happiness.

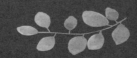

ST. MOTHER TERESA

Teach me, dear Lord,
to sit at your feet
daily and love you
extravagantly!

RUTH HARMS CALKIN

You are worthy, O Lord our God, to receive glory and honor and power. For you created all things, and they exist because you created what you pleased.

REVELATION 4:11

Let all who take refuge in you rejoice; let
them sing joyful praises forever. Spread
your protection over them, that all who love
your name may be filled with joy. For you
bless the godly, O LORD; you surround them
with your shield of love.

PSALM 5:11-12

The end of the world is coming soon. Therefore, **be earnest and disciplined in your prayers.**

1 PETER 4:7

Restore us,
O God; make your
face shine on us,
that we may be saved.

PSALM 80:3, NIV

This prayer was sung by the prophet
Habakkuk: I have heard all about you, LORD.
I am filled with awe by your amazing works.
In this time of our deep need, help us again
as you did in years gone by. And in your
anger, remember your mercy.

HABAKKUK 3:1-2

Fill Thou my life,
O Lord my God, in
ev'ry part with praise,
that my whole being
may proclaim Thy
being and Thy ways.

HORATIUS BONAR

Come, O Lord, in
much mercy down into
my soul, and
*take possession
and dwell there.*

ST. AUGUSTINE

You, dear friends, must build each other up in your most holy faith, pray in the power of the Holy Spirit, and await the mercy of our Lord Jesus Christ, who will bring you eternal life. In this way, you will keep yourselves safe in God's love.

JUDE 1:20-21

Father God, help me to study diligently, to listen attentively, to think clearly, and to respond honestly to your Word in my quiet moments. In the name of Jesus, your Son, my Savior, I pray. Amen.

JOSH McDOWELL

Bless those who curse you. Pray for those who hurt you.

LUKE 6:28

O Lord, by all thy

dealings

with us . . .
let us be brought
to thee.

PHILLIPS BROOKS

Father, we invite you to work in our hearts today. This day would be nothing without your Spirit—convicting, convincing, encouraging, and helping us. We can do nothing on our own, and so we ask for your help in all we do.

LARRY BURKETT

Come and hear, all you who fear God; let me tell you what he has done for me. I cried out to him with my mouth; his praise was on my tongue. If I had cherished sin in my heart, the Lord would not have listened; but God has surely listened and has heard my prayer. Praise be to God, who has not rejected my prayer or withheld his love from me!

PSALM 66:16-20, NIV

The eyes of the Lord are on the righteous and his ears are attentive to their prayer.

1 PETER 3:12, NIV

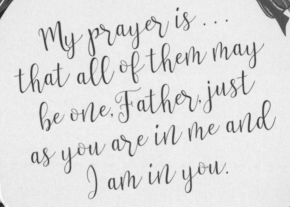

My prayer is . . .
that all of them may
be one, Father, just
as you are in me and
I am in you.

JOHN 17:20-21, NIV

Prayer can leap over oceans, speed across
burning deserts, spring over mountains,
bound through jungles, and carry the healing,
helping power of the Gospel to the object
of prayer.

BILLY GRAHAM

LIVING
EXPRESSIONS
COLLECTION

Living Expressions invites you to explore God's Word
and express your creativity in ways that are refreshing
to the spirit and restorative to the soul.

Visit Tyndale online at www.tyndale.com.

TYNDALE, Tyndale's quill logo, *Living Expressions*, and the Living Expressions logo
are registered trademarks of Tyndale House Publishers, Inc.

A Bouquet of Heartfelt Prayers to Give You Strength

Compilation copyright © 2018 by Tyndale House Publishers, Inc. All rights reserved.

Cover illustration of curly border copyright © Drew Melton/Creative Market.
All rights reserved.

Cover illustration of floral elements copyright © The Autumn Rabbit Ltd/Creative
Market. All rights reserved.

Cover photograph of watercolor texture copyright © ArtistMef/Creative Market.
All rights reserved.

Interior photographs of watercolor paper copyright © songglod/Adobe Stock.
All rights reserved.

Interior illustrations of stars garland copyright © lunalexx/Adobe Stock.
All rights reserved.

Interior illustrations of bird and florals copyright © Sukhyun/Adobe Stock.
All rights reserved.

Cover design by Cathryn Pratt. Interior design by Nicole Grimes.

Unless otherwise indicated, all Scripture quotations are taken from the *Holy Bible*,
New Living Translation, copyright © 1996, 2004, 2007, 2013, 2015 by Tyndale
House Foundation. Used by permission of Tyndale House Publishers, Inc., Carol
Stream, Illinois 60188. All rights reserved. Scripture quotations marked ESV are
taken from the *The Holy Bible*, English Standard Version® (ESV®), copyright © 2001
by Crossway, a publishing ministry of Good News Publishers. Used by permission.
All rights reserved. Scripture quotations marked KJV are taken from the *Holy
Bible*, King James Version. Scripture quotations marked NIV are taken from the
Holy Bible, *New International Version,*® *NIV.*® Copyright ©1973, 1978, 1984, 2011
by Biblica, Inc.® Used by permission. All rights reserved worldwide. Scripture
quotations marked NKJV are taken from the New King James Version,® copyright
© 1982 by Thomas Nelson, Inc. Used by permission. All rights reserved.

Every effort has been made to provide accurate source attribution for quotations in
this book. Should any attributions be found to be incorrect, the publisher welcomes
written documentation supporting correction for subsequent printings. For material
not in public domain, selection was made according to generally accepted fair use
standards and practices.

For information about special discounts for bulk purchases, please contact Tyndale
House Publishers at csresponse@tyndale.com, or call 1-800-323-9400.

ISBN 978-1-4964-3608-5

Printed in China

24	23	22	21	20	19	18
7	6	5	4	3	2	1